GW00630560

First edition published 2011 by Flare Publications and the London School of Astrology
BCM Planets, London WC1N 3XX, England, UK; Tel: 0700 2 33 44 55
www.flareuk.com and www.londonschoolofastrology.co.uk
email: admin@londonschoolofastrology.co.uk

A CIP catalogue record for this book is available from the British Library

ISBN: 978-1-903353-19-6

To contact the author, please email him at info@flareuk.com
Parts of this work have appeared in *The Astrological Journal* and *The Mountain Astrologer*
Charts calculated using Solar Fire software. Cover Photo: Hironai.

**With my thanks to Craig Knottenbelt for the cover design, June Stewart for her feedback,
and to Jane Struthers for her support and her care in proofing the text. This introductory
book is dedicated to all the students to whom I have taught Solar Arc Directions
– thank *you* for teaching me so much about them.**

By the same author:
The Frank Guide to Palm Reading (Flare, 2011, revised edition of *Palm Reading*)
The Astrology of Love, Sex & Seduction (with Fiona Graham) (Flare, 2011, rev. *Venus* and *Mars*)
Humour in the Horoscope: The Astrology of Comedy (Flare, 2011)
Palmistry 4 Today (Rider, 2002, rev. Flare, 2010)
The Astrologer's Book of Charts (Flare, 2009)
Palm Reading (Hamlyn [UK], Sterling [US], 2004)
Venus: Your Key to Love (booklet, Flare, 2000)
Mars: Your Burning Desires (booklet, Flare, 2000)
The Essentials of Hand Analysis (booklet, Flare, 1999)
British Entertainers: The Astrological Profiles (Flare, 1997, rev. 2003)
The Clifford Data Compendium (Solar Fire program, 1997, rev. 2000)

Forthcoming titles: *Getting to the Heart of Your Chart: Playing Astrological Detective*; *Seductive
Art of Palmistry*; and *The Midheaven: Spotlight on Success*

Also published by Flare Publications:
The Draconic Chart by Rev. Pamela Crane (2000; rev. 2011)
Kim Farley's Astro Mind Maps by Kim Farley (2010)
Jane Struthers' 101 Astrology Questions by Jane Struthers (2010)
The Twelve Houses by Howard Sasportas (2007)
The Contemporary Astrologer's Handbook by Sue Tompkins (2007)
Jupiter and Mercury: An A to Z by Paul Wright (2006)
Astrology in the Year Zero by Garry Phillipson (2000)
The Sun Sign Reader by Joan Revill (2000)
Shorthand of the Soul: The Quotable Horoscope by David Hayward (1999)

Solar Arc Directions

Frank C. Clifford

Part One: Try Solar Arc Directions

Let me tell you a secret: I'm passionate about Solar Arc Directions but I couldn't wait to write a complete book on forecasting to share what I've learned. Instead, I created this booklet and I'm on the starting blocks and raring to go. So are you set and ready to run with me?

Over the years, there have been books and articles written on this subject by some stellar astrologers, but I felt the need to write an 'instant' pocketbook guide – something to give you the inside track so that you can avoid certain hurdles and make use of forecasting techniques that will help you sprint to the finish line!

Adopting this method of prediction has given me a tool to spot life events and pivotal moments quickly. Solar Arc (SA) is accurate, reliable, straightforward and simple – so simple that these measurements can be made *at a glance.*

This booklet is designed to help you become familiar with this method, to spot the important years of a life quickly from a natal chart, and, with a few famous examples, see how directions can reveal and describe the unfolding of major developments and life events. In my forecasting work, I use Solar Arc Directions with transits and the lunar phases; I also find that they're excellent at the beginning of a consultation – when asking questions about key life dates – to test the accuracy of the client's birth time. Solar Arcs that occur early in life are also very useful to consider during a consultation when pinpointing and understanding patterns ('scripts') formed in childhood.

In the following nine sections, I shall focus on what directions are, how to use them and how they differ from other systems. Then, in Part 2, I'll offer up a number of examples of directions in action, and in Part 3, I'll introduce a hidden forecasting tool that works very well for my clients. By then, I hope you'll be hooked! The booklet ends with some forecasting tips in Part 4.

Introducing Directions

A day for a year...? Simply put, one rotation of the Earth's axis (which takes a day) is said to symbolize one rotation of the Earth around the Sun (a cycle that takes a year). Each day, the Sun, planets and the backdrop of signs all appear to rise (at the Ascendant), culminate (MC), set (Descendant) and anti-culminate (IC) – this diurnal (daily) movement is completed in 24 hours. And from our viewpoint, the Sun appears to move approximately one degree (i.e. 60 minutes of arc) forward through the zodiac each day. With Solar Arc, this one degree of arc (space) a day represents a year (twelve months) of time.

For every year of life, *the Sun's movement each day after birth is calculated.* How far the Sun has moved at the age in question (e.g. at age ten, the Sun would have moved approximately 10°) is then *added to all the planets and house cusps* so they all move at the same rate. (Someone born with the Sun at 5° Taurus will have a Solar Arc Directed Sun at 15° at age ten.) We then consider and interpret the aspects (e.g. conjunction, opposition) that the newly directed planets make to the original, natal chart. (That ten-year old might have a natal planet, such as Jupiter, at 15° Scorpio. At age ten, they would have the following direction: <u>SA Sun opposite natal Jupiter</u>. By then, their own SA Jupiter would also have moved the same ten degrees and have a directed position of 25° Scorpio, on its way to meet/aspect other planets.)

To interpret a direction, we would consider keywords and the symbolism of the directed planet and its effect on the planet located in the natal chart (taking into account the person's age, awareness and context) – see Part 4.

The two most common types of directions in current use are:

1. One Degree: The positions in the birth chart are all moved forwards by exactly 1° for every year of life (regardless of the exact daily motion of the Sun). For example, to plot the directed positions of a chart of someone aged 32 years and 6 months, move the entire chart forwards by 32°30' (half a degree = half a year).

2. Solar Arc: Again, using the one-day-equals-one-year principle, the planetary positions and angles of the birth chart are directed forwards by the *actual* distance (arc) the Sun has transited each day after birth, which is usually very close to (but not exactly) 1° (it ranges from 57' to 1°01').

On the face of it, there appears to be little difference between these methods but, as we shall see later, because the daily rate of the Sun differs slightly throughout the year, there are likely to be some discrepancies the older one gets. In this book, we will be looking chiefly at the second method, Solar Arc.

But how do they differ from Secondary Progressions? Day-for-a-year Secondary Progressions take the ephemeris as its guideline (e.g. the planetary positions in the ephemeris <u>30 days</u> after birth equate to the progressed positions at <u>30 years</u> of age), so each planet will progress at its own rate. During those 30 days, the Moon would have moved through the entire zodiac, while the outer planets may have only moved by 1° at most.

With Solar Arc, *everything (including each of the four angles) moves forwards at the same rate* – that of the daily transiting Sun.[1] Unlike progressions, directions are not based on movements in the heavens (i.e. actual movements recorded in an ephemeris). Solar Arc Directions are a *symbolic* way of moving the chart to forecast/predict, and not as popular with astrologers as Secondary Progressions, but there are many advantages to using them with (or, preferably, as a substitute for) progressions.

As a beginner, I was never in love with progressions. I always wanted a predictive tool that would give me results fast – something I could work out quickly while glancing at the horoscope. It must have been a fellow Aries who prayed, 'Lord give me patience... but hurry!' So when I discovered Solar Arcs for myself (in fact, like a good Aries, I thought I *had* discovered them – period!), I ran with them and saw how useful they could be in tracking major life events.

Once in a Lifetime Happenings

Whereas transits are part of larger cycles, showing 'trends' and life developments, and reflecting the waxing and waning (and repetition) of cyclical aspects of our lives, each major Solar Arc Direction (e.g. SA Mercury conjunct Venus) occurs only once in a lifetime and many specific aspects won't ever occur if the planets/angles are too far from one another.

For an exact aspect to reoccur (e.g. a conjunction), we would need to live to at least 360 years old! Even exact sextiles (60°) to the same planet/point would only occur again after approximately 120 years. Repetitions of the minor aspects (such as the semi-sextile or semi-square) are possible in a lifetime (from approximately age 60 and 90 respectively).

So, being essentially one-off occurrences, Solar Arc Directions can be seen as key stages ('saddle points') in our lives, symbolizing the *unfolding of the chart* as it is directed forward by the rate of the Sun (itself a symbol of life development and its unfolding). The Solar Arc Directions in our lifetime (particularly the conjunctions, squares and oppositions) show the milestones on our journey towards the discovery of *who we are meant/were born to be* and towards *fulfilling our life purpose(s)*. This is, in essence, the Solar principle.

Aspects and Orbs

With Solar Arc, the conjunction and major hard aspects (square and opposition) between the planets (and four angles) are the most significant. These are energetic aspects that tend to 'manifest' more as concrete life events and dynamic turning points. Some astrologers add the trine, sextile and 'minor' aspects, which increases the likelihood of more directions occurring each year. Other astrologers, such as Noel Tyl (who has written at great length on the subject), use a set of midpoints too, and offer interpretations based on more specific measurements (directions to the Sun–Moon midpoint, for instance). I tend to stick with the major aspects in Solar Arc and use these with transits and lunar phases.

It is recommended that you use up to half a degree either side of an aspect (which equates to approximately six months leading up to exactitude and six months following it). In his work on the subject (which includes the major treatise *Solar Arcs*), Tyl reminds us that, rather than providing us with a wider time frame – a get-out clause to get our prediction 'right' – orbs are about the *gradual realization of a process*. I would argue that events themselves may happen in a split second, but looking deeper, there are usually meanings, feelings and associations that have been building up beforehand that also last beyond any particular 'event' or moment of time.

The Speed of the Sun

The Sun moves at different speeds during the year. This information can be found in *Raphael's Astronomical Ephemeris,* published annually by Foulsham, and usually appears on pages 26-28. These speeds differ very slightly from year to year. Let's examine the Sun's daily motion (i.e. its speed in degrees, minutes and seconds) at the first day of each month of 2011.

1 January: 1°01'10"	1 May: 0°58'16"	1 September: 0°58'04"
1 February: 1°00'56"	1 June: 0°57'32"	1 October: 0°59'00"
1 March: 1°00'15"	1 July: 0°57'14"	1 November: 1°00'02"
1 April: 0°59'15"	1 August: 0°57'25"	1 December 1°00'49"

The Sun is at its slowest in late June/early July (approx. 0°57'12") and at its fastest at the turn of the year (approx. 1°01'11"). Noel Tyl offers a way to remember this: the Sun's rate is slow in the hot, balmy summer (when we take life at a more leisurely pace) and the Sun's rate is fast in the cold winter (when we need to speed up to keep from freezing). Well, it's a helpful analogy for those of us in the Northern Hemisphere who experience summer between June and August.

The Sun's pace is exactly 1° per day only in early March and late October/ early November. It is possible, then, that those born at other times in the year have directed horoscopes that have either lost ground (especially May–August births) or raced ahead of their age (especially December–January births). For example, if we were born with the Sun in Gemini, Cancer or Leo, the Sun moves slower (57' a day), so by 10 years old the cumulative daily motion of the Sun means that the Sun has lost up to 30 minutes of arc (half a degree) from what we might expect – i.e. by age 10, everything has been directed 9°30' instead of an estimated 10°. By age 50 (when, by the One Degree method, everything has moved forward 50°) it is possible to have lost almost 2°30' of arc (i.e. the chart has only moved 47°30').

The Sun in Sagittarius, Capricorn or Aquarius moves faster than 1° a day, so at age 50, the chart will be directed further than estimated (about 50°50').

To reiterate this point: those born with the Sun in Sagittarius, Capricorn or Aquarius will reach 50° of arc faster (and at an earlier age) than someone with the Sun in a 'slower' sign (Gemini, Cancer or Leo).

So, it is usually enough to estimate by eye how far a chart has directed by simply knowing the client's age, but in extreme cases and over the years the estimate and the actual movement may be out by a few degrees. This makes a big difference in forecasting when we consider that 1° in the chart equals one year of life. Keep this is mind – or let your computer program do it for you!

The following chart is useful in estimating how far planets/points have moved over a particular period of time:

1° = 1 year of life	40' = 8 months	20' = 4 months
55' = 11 months	35' = 7 months	15' = 3 months
50' = 10 months	30' = 6 months	10' = 2 months
45' = 9 months	25' = 5 months	5' = 1 month
	and 1' = 7-8 days	

Solar Arcs in Rectification

Due to the slowness, predictability and accuracy of Solar Arc, it is clear why this system is often used to fine-tune an approximate birth time, especially when planets aspect or pass over (conjunct) the four angles (or when the ASC–DSC or MC–IC axis aspects or passes over natal planets).

Transits move backwards and forwards over a position (sometimes up to five hits within a 1° orb), and this process can last a few years. Solar Arcs happen once only and, given a 30' orb either side of exactitude, it is easier to pinpoint sensitive degrees in the horoscope and use these to rectify the chart. If the astrologer is looking to forecast, it is often difficult to pinpoint when an 'event' (if any) will manifest during this period by looking at the transit alone. This is where one-off, forward-moving directions can help, particularly if the orb is tightened to less than 30'.

Natal Aspects Between Planets/Angles Remain the Same

With Solar Arc, every planet/angle moves forwards at the same daily rate[2] – even if that planet is retrograde in the natal chart. This is a cumulative rate (i.e. if we were born on 1 February, we add the daily rate of the Sun on the next day and so on to every point in the chart, for every year of our life). So, all the aspects in the natal chart will remain the same in the Solar Arc Directed chart. Directed planets move forwards and make aspects to natal planets/angles but will not change their relationship with each other. A Moon–Saturn conjunction (with an orb of 3°51') will always be conjunct by that same orb as both planets are directed at the same speed through the years.

This brings us to an important point: when there are close aspects in the horoscope, e.g. a tight Moon–Uranus opposition with an orb of 0°34', then as this opposition is directed, both planets will come into contact with a third (natal) planet. This third planet will be aspected by one directed planet, followed by another some 34' of arc later. For example, if the directed Moon conjuncts natal Saturn, Uranus will also oppose Saturn around the same time (34' of arc, either roughly 7 months earlier or later, depending on the planetary sequence). The same 'double whammy' occurs when any planet directs to aspect the natal Moon–Uranus opposition.

Solar Arc Directions... at a Glance

I often begin by looking at planets that are close to each other (within say 60°) and counting the degrees between them. It certainly helps to remember that there are 30 degrees per sign and 60 minutes of arc in each degree! It can be a little daunting thinking of every possible combination, but spotting planets that will conjunct in a lifetime is the best place to start, or taking one planet and seeing the major aspects it makes as it travels through a sign. After a while, you'll start seeing the horoscope as a group of planets that are, in reality, all in *some* relationship to each other by a particular number of degrees. The degrees that separate the two planets correspond (approximately) to the year of life when a merging of those two planetary energies manifests and the potential is realized. Remember that, with directions, it's always the planet at the earlier degree that will conjunct the planet positioned later. This is one aspect of 'fate' as seen in our

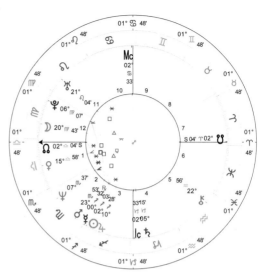

horoscope: *from the moment of our birth, the horoscope is fixed and set to unfold in a particular order of Solar Arc Directions that are unique to us.*

Let's use the birth chart of former political leader **Charles Kennedy** (chart pictured above and opposite). He was born in late November when the Sun moves approximately 1°00'40" (slightly faster than the One Degree method of estimation), so over the years the Solar Arc Directions will have moved slightly further in degrees than his age (e.g. at age 60, the directions will be around 61 degrees further than their natal positions). It is useful to keep this in mind.

To train the eye, start with a planet near one of the four angles. There are two planets either side of his Ascendant (ASC). Let's start with the Moon, which is at 20°43' Virgo. The Ascendant is 1°48' Libra. There are just over 11° between the two points. So, moving all of the positions forwards, we would say that just after his 11th birthday, Charles had <u>SA Moon conjunct natal ASC</u>, i.e. his Moon directed towards his Ascendant at that particular age. (His SA Ascendant at this age would also have moved one degree for every year of life, and be standing somewhere around 12° Libra.) At age 11, there was a meeting of planetary energies, and we can expect some Moon–Ascendant symbolism (in the form of an event or process) to have taken place.

What about Venus? It stands at 15°58' Libra. If directed forwards through the zodiac, Venus will never reach the Ascendant in Charles's lifetime, but the Ascendant *will* reach Venus by Solar Arc. But at what age? The Ascendant is 1°48' Libra and Venus is 14°10' ahead of it in the zodiac. So, just after the age of 14, Charles will have <u>SA ASC conjunct natal Venus</u>.

Here, for simplicity, we are making a rough estimate based upon One Degree, but a computer will tell us the exact date that the directed Moon moved on to the Ascendant and when the Ascendant directed to form a conjunction with Venus.

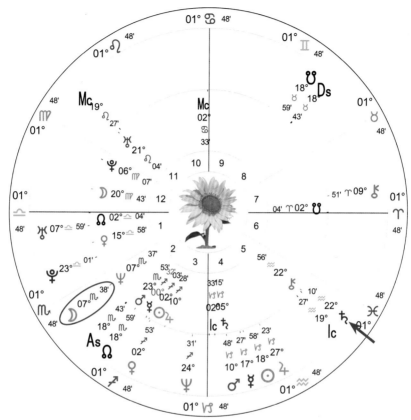

Neptune stands at 7°37' Scorpio, just shy of 36° away from the Ascendant (the distance from 1°48' Libra to 7°37' Scorpio). So, Solar Arc ASC conjunct natal Neptune will occur at around the age of 36.

It is possible to find the arc between each of the planets and angles and work out when they would meet (conjunct) each other. Some, of course, will never form a conjunction during a natural lifetime, but we should also be looking at the other aspects (such as the square and opposition).

For greater accuracy, I would always use Solar Arc rather than One Degree Directions. (An astrology program or an ephemeris for the year of birth will help with this.) As we've already noted in Charles Kennedy's case, because he was born in late November there is little difference between the One Degree method and Solar Arc.

Let's look at the difference for the date of **7 January 2006** (the outer wheel of the bi-wheel, pictured above). On this date, Charles is 46 years, 1 month and 2 weeks old. By the One Degree method, everything would have moved 46°07' (46 years = 46°, 1 month = 5', 2 weeks = approx. 2'). But by Solar Arc, everything has moved almost 46°55'. Not much difference, it seems, but in terms of accuracy, those 48' equate to almost 10 months in real, calendar time.

On 7 January 2006, Charles Kennedy resigned as Leader of the Liberal Democrats, two days after admitting that a serious drinking habit (much rumoured in the Press) was affecting his health, productivity and reputation. By Solar Arc, the Moon had reached an exact conjunction with his natal Neptune.

The important point to remember is that the active planet – the one directing and on the move – is the planet that *brings its energy and symbolism* (based on its basic meaning as well as natal set-up) *to the natal planet*. It acts as the verb that affects or comes into contact with a particular aspect of our character (as seen by the natal planet's placement). For example, the Sun 'illuminates', 'spotlights', 'highlights'; the Moon 'instinctively feels to the need to...' and 'takes care' and 'comforts'; Mercury opens a door of communication to 'express', 'articulate', 'connect', 'find patterns' and 'formulate'.

Natally, Kennedy's Moon (habits/dependency) is in the 12th House (secrets/undoing/the uncontrollable and unruly areas of ourselves that can run riot) in the sign of Virgo (health/efficiency). It rules the MC (reputation) and the earthy 10th Equal House (EQHS). Neptune (alcohol/addiction/scandal/resignation) is in the 2nd House and rules the 6th House (both 'Earth' houses related to the body and work routine/health respectively). Interestingly, his Party had spent much of the past five years concealing his battle with the bottle. Kennedy had sought professional help in 2002 when Solar Arc Neptune squared his natal Moon – his addiction (Neptune) had reached crisis point (square) which brought an attempt (square) to get healthy and to restructure his daily life (Moon in Virgo).

Another Solar Arc is fast approaching: SA Saturn conjunct Chiron in Aquarius in the 5th. Drinking is a major part of socializing for MPs in the Commons. This direction could suggest sobering up (Saturn) and the end of partying (5th) with his peer group (Aquarius) – fun (5th) that had caused him much harm (Chiron).

Apart from a few inner planet 'triggers' to his natal and directed charts, *there were no outer planet transits* (using tight orbs) at this time. This is a reminder to have more than transits in your forecasting toolkit, and to always begin forecasting by looking at the individual's character, personality and temperament (as shown by planets on angles, the Ascendant and Moon, respectively), as well as motivations (elemental imbalances) and modes of behaviour (modal imbalances).

As well as aspects from the directed chart to the natal chart, consider the importance of planets that direct into a new sign by Solar Arc (approx. every 30 years) and move into a new house of the horoscope. A planet that has directed to the final degree of a sign will often bring crisis-driven issues to the fore that are specifically related to that sign/planet combination. Sometimes these are last-minute repeats of old patterns, which serve as reminders to let go of particular behaviour. But when the planet (or angle) crosses over to the next sign, there's an awareness of switching approach, and we may encounter a fresh opportunity to experience a new quality to that planet. More of this later.

Some Further Considerations

Solar Arc Directions are said to be more event-orientated than Secondary Progressions, showing more mundane and concrete happenings. It is arguable, though, that because dynamic, event-based aspects (conjunction, square and opposition) are used chiefly with Solar Arc, we are likely to see these directions as actual manifestations of events. Secondary Progressions are said to be more internal and subtle in their influences, unfolding at each planet's own speed, reflecting the client's 'inner psychological climate'; they are less likely to 'coincide' with actual events.

It is said that a Solar Arc Direction (like a progression) waits for a trigger from a transiting planet before an 'event' occurs, but I've seen countless dramatic (and highly descriptive) Solar Arcs occurring at times of significant events and yet there's been an absence of corresponding, meaningful transits. I've also noticed that the more major directions we have during a year, the more dramatic or life-changing that year often is.

There is no point in reading a directed chart on its own, as a constructed Solar Arc chart will look very similar to the natal chart; planets will be found in the same houses and aspects to each other, but in different signs. On the other hand, a Secondary Progressed chart can be analysed on its own.

Finally, it is also possible to connect events and periods in the life by linking transits to the natal chart with later transits to the directed chart. For example, the Saturn Return occurs at 29 but transiting Saturn catches up with SA Saturn some two to three years later. This 'Shadow' Saturn Return repeats issues that emerged during the Saturn Return but they are of a different quality (sign position) and usually in a different area of life (house position). It's a second chance to complete the unfinished business of our late 20s. I'll be introducing this later.

What We've Just Learned... in a Nutshell

1. With Solar Arc, one degree (60 minutes) of arc equals approximately one year of time (so 5' of arc equals 1 month). The natal planetary positions and angles are directed forwards by the actual distance the Sun has transited each day after birth; this is usually very close to 1° but there are slight seasonal variations (up to 1°01' at the turn of the year, as slow as 0°57'–0°58' from May to August, and very close to 1° in March and October/November).

2. Everything in the chart is directed forwards at the same rate. A Solar Arc chart will look the same as a natal chart except every point will have moved forwards approximately one degree for every year of life (i.e. the aspects in the chart remain but the chart moves forwards through the signs and houses); very 'tight' natal aspects (with an orb under one degree) give rise to 'double whammies', where an aspect combination (e.g. Sun square Mars) directs to hit a natal position in the same year.

3. With all points moving approximately one degree a year, no Solar Arc direction (using major, Ptolemaic aspects) can be repeated in a lifetime; directions are one-off occurrences, saddle points in our lives.

4. Starting off, it is best to focus on the conjunction, square and opposition, allowing a half-degree orb either side of exactitude (this is equivalent to six months before and after the exact hit). Study your own chart retrospectively by looking at key events in your life and see how the symbolism of a direction describes the events and, in particular, the feelings, actions and repercussions associated with these events. Or you may prefer to take one planet at a time and track the aspects it makes at particular years in the lifetime.

5. It is possible to fine-tune the horoscope by using directions to and from the four angles to test possible alternative birth times.

6. A planet or angle directing from a sign (29°) into a new sign (0°) is an important period of change; so are directions over house cusps, if the birth time is accurate.

7. There are powerful links between a transit to a natal position (e.g. TR Saturn to the Sun) and the same, later transit to the Solar Arc position (e.g. TR Saturn to the directed Sun). This is named a 'Shadow Transit'.

 # Part Two: Directions in Action

To demonstrate the simplicity and accuracy of Solar Arc Directions, I have picked out some charts that interest me from my book, *The Astrologer's Book of Charts*, and then researched a few key dates for each example. The data are from birth certificates, hospital records or birth announcements – as accurate as we're likely to get.

First Steps

At the LSA, I tend to stress a number of points when forecasting with the natal chart. Firstly, in my experience, transits and directions describe the processes, feelings and reactions rather than the actual event. This is one of the reasons why, when using a method of prediction, the timing of actual events can be 'off'. For example, a relationship break-up can affect us on many levels and may extend many years (from an early decision to split through to the eventual moving on after the break-up). The precise date of parting might not be 'seen' by transits or directions, etc., but other stages in this process may be of greater importance to the person (and thus more obvious in transits, directions, etc.).

With some context, we can usually understand the area in which the event will play out, and the types of situation the planet in question can 'give birth to', but arguably it is more the astrologer's job to pinpoint the cycle/planetary period, articulate the processes taking place and to 'speak' in a way in which the client can hear and apply this information. On a psychological level we must ask: what is being brought forward for the client to explore? There are too many external variables (culture, gender, society, education, time in history, etc.) to assume that the chart provides all the details and answers to our future. With forecasting, much depends on our ability to understand the client's natal horoscope; in this we can see their life stories (particularly in their major aspects and configurations), and patterns of behaviour, viewpoints and a range of reactions to various situations (essentially the Moon and Ascendant complexes).

Ingresses

I've noticed that when a planet enters a new sign (what's known as an ingress) it connects and 'speaks' to any planet or angle in that sign – regardless of degree. For example, transiting Pluto's ingress into Capricorn has a strong effect on any planet/point we have in that sign (and any other sign it makes a major aspect to). This forms the basis of predicting with Whole Sign Houses. For example, from my observations, someone with a Capricorn Ascendant is already experiencing an Ascendant-type of Pluto transformation – regardless of the Ascendant's actual degree. Pluto is, of course, most potent – and its symbolism clearest – when within a degree of a planet's position, but its journey through the sign has a strong bearing on any planet/angle in the sign.

In some ways, it is similar with directions. By Solar Arc, planets take thirty years to travel through a sign, so sign changes are eventful, transitional times. As a planet ingresses, it automatically enters a new element and mode, and this would indicate a new attitude, a new style and motivation – particularly noticeable during the first year/degree. The natal planet has the opportunity to speak a different language (new sign) and to connect with new 'people' in the horoscope (the ruler of that sign or any planets posited).[3]

I would go as far as to say that the whole first degree (0°) would indicate a year of getting to know and beginning to experience the essence of that sign (and the messages of natal planets we have placed here). In some ways it's a portent – a signpost indicating much of what we can expect for the next thirty years condensed into the first twelve months. My astrologer-friend in Boston, Fernando Guimaraes, suggests the first degree is like an 'operatic overture' – an introduction that sets the mood for what follows. The experience is heightened during this first year, and the remaining twenty-nine years are eventful in this respect only when triggered by aspect to other planets/points along its journey. Additional information about the 'first degree experience' will come from the house in which 0° of this sign falls. And, as I've said, by entering the new sign it will immediately connect to any planets we have in that sign (even if they are placed in the next house).

Babe-Watch: The Flash of a Smile

Take for example the directed Sun. Among other things, this acts as a giant spotlight on the area it is directing through and illuminates/brings to light our creative potential. The Sun is the essence of who we were born to be, our calling – the area of life that is significant, meaningful and makes us feel alive.

Here's an example of astrology in action that made me chuckle. *Playboy* pin-up and model-actress **Pamela Anderson** (bi-wheel pictured opposite, directions set for **1 September 1989**) was discovered in the summer of 1989 while at a football match (I haven't found the exact date but biography tells us that she was still twenty-one, suggesting it occurred prior to her birthday on 1 July). Suddenly the stadium screen zoomed in on Anderson, who was wearing a tight T-shirt with the logo of a beer company on it. The young blonde model was cheered and then brought down to the field to receive the crowd's further ovation! Following another similar event, the beer company had the sense to hire her and this led to her first cover shoot for *Playboy* magazine (the October 1989 issue).

With the natal Sun in Cancer, Pamela Anderson epitomizes the modern girl next door... the Barbie doll with huge breast implants – modern-day weapons of mass distraction. What is telling about her Solar Arc positions for 1989 is that her Sun was moving into Leo that summer, just after her discovery and at the exact time she was being photographed for her first *Playboy* cover. This brought her notice and publicity, demonstrated in the most blatant of Leonine imagery: the centrefold. By emerging into the sign of Leo, the Sun became very prominent and was in immediate 'dialogue' with two planets in that sign: Jupiter and Venus (together, they could be said to symbolize her mass popularity as a pneumatic sex symbol). The directed Moon in Taurus was also exactly trine Pluto, suggestive of her 'baring all', her mass appeal and some major financial opportunities, too.

As an aside, is her sudden discovery written in the natal horoscope? Uranus–MC aspects are seen in the charts of those whose reputations change overnight and are in the right place at the right time (or perhaps in the wrong place at the wrong time). Anderson has Uranus co-ruling the MC and in quincunx to it. With a natal quincunx, the plot changes – whether we like it or not. And Neptune–MC aspects can suggest a lack of awareness of how we're perceived by others in our social or professional lives, and it can also give us a reputation for being glamorous, photogenic, sleazy or otherworldly. Anderson has Neptune square her Aquarian MC and square her Venus in Leo, which describes her image as a big-haired glamourpuss as well as her dual career pursuits: aside from her modelling/acting, she is an activist for PETA (People for the Ethical Treatment of Animals), an organization that fights to alleviate animal suffering.

Interestingly, her Moon directed to oppose Neptune three years later – the time she joined the cast of *Baywatch* (her first episode aired on 20 September 1992). The TV show about glamorous beach lifeguards (note both planets involved) would make her a global sensation (Neptune's job is to mass-market, sell and

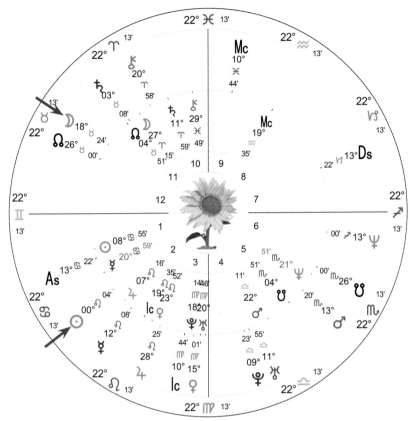

disseminate to everyone). At the same time, Venus (natally in Leo) conjunct Pluto to suggest the huge impact she was about to make as a sex symbol. And what of the tumultuous and violent marriage to Tommy Lee and the infamous sex tape that circulated on the Internet? The marriage dissolved in 1998, around the time the sex tape was leaked, causing a media frenzy – Neptune (natally in Scorpio and square to Venus in Leo) had directed to Anderson's Descendant.

The Final Degree

Another consideration is when a planet directs to the last degree of a sign (29°). During that year, we tend to experience the most challenging aspects of the sign, particularly if it is relatively 'foreign' to us or if we have not taken care to understand/integrate its essence (after all, this degree reveals the cumulative effects of that planet/angle's experiences through the sign). This final degree appears to have a sting in the tail: although we are poised for change, we have to attend to areas ruled by that sign before we are able to move on. I started to see this with clients who felt (or were rendered) impotent in some way in the areas/

themes linked to the sign. There can be times when we feel 'in the dark' about these areas, or we have an urgent need to confront them 'before it's too late'.

Consider the Taurus/Scorpio polarity. Both are signs of potency, linked to the processes of attachment and accumulation, as well the exploration of physical and emotional pleasure and possession. One client had her Ascendant ('surroundings', 'horizon', 'environment') directed to the end of Scorpio in her 2nd House and experienced huge financial instability (a Scorpionic crisis and near wipe-out). Before it left Scorpio it made a trine (by Solar Arc) to her Moon and, under additional aspects and transits, she experienced the release (trine) of her elderly mother passing away. The following year, the directed Ascendant moved into Sagittarius and immediately conjunct Jupiter, offering a major relocation plus financial opportunities from abroad.

Another client divorced as Venus directed towards the end of Taurus (in her 12th House). At the final degree, she had to pay her spouse a large sum of money in a divorce settlement – one that she felt was unfair and unjustified. Although this did not force a financial crisis, it did limit her future options (Venus is less to do with 'money' than being concerned with the perks, luxuries and privileges that extra money can bestow).

Take a look at the biographies and key events that follow and see how these are illustrated by relevant and meaningful Solar Arc Directions.

A Right Royal Example

Royal charts are over-used, so I tend to avoid them in articles and books. But **Prince Harry**'s Solar Arc Directions (pictured opposite in a bi-wheel) speak so beautifully at a time of such personal tragedy: the death of his mother. Around the date (**31 August 1997**), Harry had no significant transits or progressions, yet we note a few highly influential and meaningful directions.

Firstly, at his mother's death, Neptune was one minute from a partile (exact) conjunction to his Ascendant. We can speculate, as he approached adolescence, that this must have been a highly disorientating time for the young prince. In addition to his own sadness, he encountered an unprecedented wave of national grief and mass mourning (Neptune) that swept the UK. In his birth chart, Neptune originates from the 12th House in Sagittarius and squares the Sun in Virgo. Someone with the Sun square Neptune may not have the clearest sense of who their father is, what they were born to do or what their role should be; William and Harry have been labelled 'the heir and the spare'.

At the time of Diana's death, Solar Arc Uranus was approaching – four months from partile – a square to his Virgo Sun. Harry's subsequent 'searching for himself' and provocative behaviour provided much fodder for the tabloids and may have much to do with these landmark directions of Neptune–Ascendant and Uranus square Sun, as well as a natal Mars–Uranus conjunction in Sagittarius.

Although we're not privy to the reactions and innermost thoughts of the royal family (and perhaps we should be thankful for small mercies), the astrology of that event is highly meaningful. At the time of the car crash, the rulers of Harry's MC and IC (the axis showing the parental influence on formative years and the subsequent emergence into society) met by Solar Arc Direction. Venus (having just entered Scorpio) formed a conjunction to Pluto at 0° Scorpio. This was no bountiful Venus–Jupiter direction! It was the violent death of his beloved, radiant mother who was in full bloom and developing independence. (Harry's Venus rules the IC and disposits the Moon in Taurus.) The natal MC in Scorpio is indicative of a 'heavy duty' life direction that is marked and shaped by major transition or transformation (often the death of a mentor/parent). Note, too, that the MC had directed to the final degree of Scorpio (conjunct the South Node).

His brother William's chart shows Mars fast approaching Pluto by direction (both planets rule his MC). Mars, like Harry's Venus, is natally in Libra. Interestingly, William's directed Ascendant reached 11° Capricorn (Harry's Rising degree) at this time, perhaps bringing the brothers much closer at this time of loss. Finally, Solar Arc Saturn directed into Scorpio (joining his MC and Jupiter in that sign) two days after Diana's death.

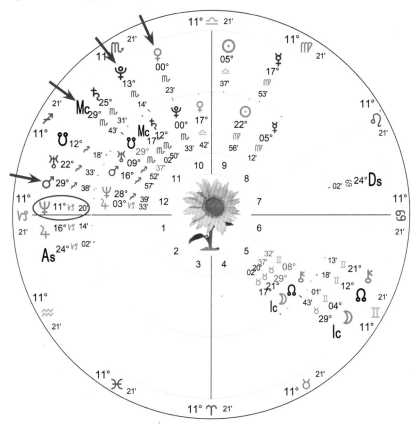

Prince Charles had transiting Uranus on his Descendant when ex-wife Diana died, but when the announcement of their separation was made some time back on 9 December 1992, Solar Arc Mars was on his Descendant in Aquarius (semi-square its natal position in Sagittarius in the 5th). SA Chiron went on to square his MC soon after, the IC conjunct Chiron in the 4th, and the 4th House cusp conjunct Mars in Sagittarius: the scene was set for some damage to his credibility as heir and the weakening of his reputation, as both camps took off their gloves and fought via the media. Interestingly, Solar Arc Pluto was opposite his natal Aries MC during the brief lead-up to his civil ceremony with former mistress Camilla Parker Bowles. There was some nervousness among royal-watchers as to how the marriage would affect the status (MC) of the future king.

Taking a Stand

In early 1964, Cassius Clay began meeting with the controversial, charismatic leader Malcolm X. It's not known precisely when Clay first embraced Islam but on the night of **6 March 1964**, Clay was renamed **Muhammad Ali** (bi-wheel opposite, set for this date) and officially became a member of the Nation of Islam. This move provoked much outrage of its own and Ali once stated, 'We who follow the teachings of Elijah Muhammad don't want to be forced to integrate. Integration is wrong. We don't want to live with the white man; that's all.'

At this time, the Sun (ruling his Leo Ascendant) directed over the Descendant in Aquarius. This is indicative of Ali renaming himself and changing his identity – Sun to the ASC/DSC axis – and embracing a new 'father' (Sun) and community (Aquarius). Malcolm X's widow, Betty Shabazz, said, '[Malcolm] felt his job was to get this young man [Ali] to believe in himself and stand squarely on both feet with his shoulders back.' His daughter, Attallah Shabazz, said, '[Ali] underwent a social and political awakening... [and joined] a family of supporters.'

On 25 February 1964, a week before the official conversion, the motor-mouth braggart dethroned the World Heavyweight Champion Sonny Liston and declared cockily, 'I am the greatest!' (Jupiter). Ali's Equal 10th House cusp (not his MC) had directed to an exact conjunction with Jupiter in Gemini in the 10th (i.e. the SA Ascendant – 90° to the Equal 10th cusp – squared Jupiter). Soon after his victory and conversion, commentators were wondering whether Ali's chief role was as a Heavyweight Champion or a religious crusader (Jupiter).

One of the reasons I use Equal Houses (EQHS) is to give importance to the 10th and 4th House cusps (the nonagesimal and nadir, respectively) when using directions (or transits, for that matter). So often, the 10th and 4th House cusps speak of actual work (10th) and home matters (4th). The 10th House is the job, the career. The MC and IC speak of our reputation and our roots, and the actualization in society (MC) of deep-rooted principles embedded in childhood (IC). Most charts (unless births are near the Equator or the Ascendant is around Pisces/Aries or Virgo/Libra) have a 10th House cusp and MC that are some distance away from each other. A direction to or from the 10th House cusp

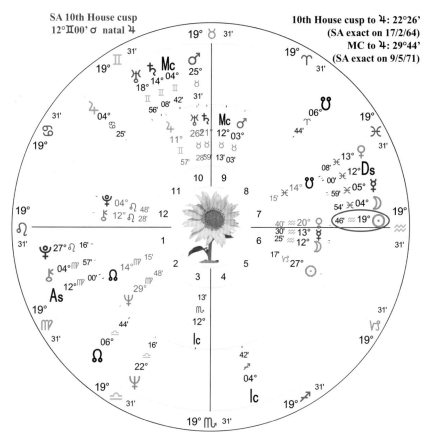

SA 10th House cusp
12°♊00' ♂ natal ♃

10th House cusp to ♃: 22°26'
(SA exact on 17/2/64)
MC to ♃: 29°44'
(SA exact on 9/5/71)

degree is a new chapter in our life path or our work. A direction to or from the MC degree speaks more of a fundamental change in our reputation and how we impact our outer environment (and how it impacts us).

In early 1971, the MC directed to that same Jupiter in Gemini in the 10th, some seven years after the 10th cusp had done so (note that his MC and 10th House cusps are seven degrees apart). Ali suffered his first-ever professional loss (to Joe Frazier, 8 March 1971) in 'The Fight of the Century', one of the most famous and publicized (Jupiter) matches of all time. Ali had been away from the ring for a number of years because of his stance against the Vietnam War. It was headlined as an anti-establishment (Ali) vs. conservative/pro-Vietnam (Frazier) match and, although he lost, Ali won the respect of the American public.

But more importantly, this SA MC conjunct Jupiter reflected an important moral victory for Ali while this aspect was still in orb three months later. Ali had declared himself a conscientious objector and been arrested and stripped of his title in April 1967. He was found guilty by jury of draft evasion, but in the four years of appeals that followed, support for Ali and condemnation of the Vietnam War had grown. Finally, on 28 June 1971 – with directed MC to Jupiter – the Supreme Court reversed his conviction (incidentally, Jupiter is retrograde). Natally, with the MC in Taurus (and Mars nearby), Ali was known for his steadfastness in the face of opposition and bigotry. When that MC reached Jupiter, it wasn't a professional victory as it had been in 1964, when the 10th House cusp (career) conjunct Jupiter. It was linked to a defining event that shaped his reputation (MC) as a man who stuck stubbornly to his principles (Taurus) and beliefs (Jupiter).

The MTV President

The chart for a president's inauguration is important, but the president's birth chart itself reflects the America that he comes to represent during his term in office. The America during the Nixon and Bush Junior administrations was as paranoid as its leaders' Mercury–Pluto aspects, while the Venusian- and Neptunian-tinged charts of charismatic presidents Clinton and Kennedy reflect the scandal-hungry American public of the 90s (fed on details of the former's salacious love life), and America's early 60s idealism (encapsulated by John and Jackie's Camelot).

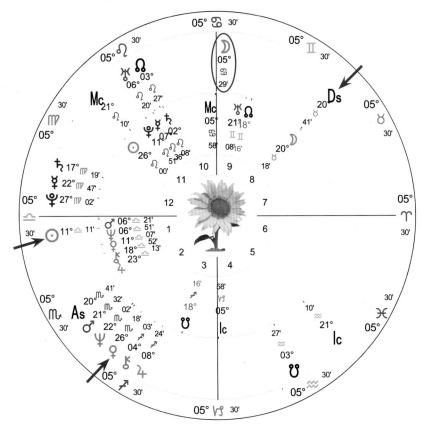

In addition, the transits and directions under which a president is elected say much about his term of office: its themes, effectiveness and response from the public. **Bill Clinton** was sworn in on **20 January 1993** (bi-wheel opposite), when Solar Arc Moon was directing into the 10th House and fast approaching his MC. The natal Moon (ruling the MC/10th) is in Taurus in his 8th House. At the same time, the directed Sun was conjunct Venus in Libra in the 1st, Venus moved to square his Sun (Scorpio to Leo) and the Descendant reached his natal Moon.

All these were indicative of Venus/Libra and Moon/Taurus times ahead – the informal, charismatic and likeable man, the hip MTV President who played saxophone, the health care reform plan, economic expansion and a federal surplus, the election slogan of 'putting people first', and the promotion of women to key jobs in his Administration. And it is not surprising that his terms of office were tainted by revelations of his sexual misconduct, or, more to the point, his denials of extra-marital affairs and the witch-hunt to remove him from office (note that Venus is natally conjunct belligerent Mars and scandalous, boundaryless Neptune). Clinton was, of course, impeached for obstruction of justice but acquitted.

Black Pearl

After two decades of hits, the classy singer Dionne Warwick (once known as the 'Black Pearl') became a key fundraiser for AIDS research. The recording that raised money and gave Warwick her biggest hit was entitled 'That's What Friends Are For' (Aquarius), a Grammy Award-winning collaboration with Elton John, Stevie Wonder and Gladys Knight. The song reached the summit of the US charts on 18 January 1986, when her directed Sun (natally in Sagittarius) was conjunct her MC in humanitarian-themed Aquarius. This led to a high profile stint as Ambassador for various US administrations. As a combination, the friendly, accessible signs of Sagittarius and Aquarius are concerned with envisioning a more ideal future, as well as opening channels of communication to reach out to humanity, erode prejudice and break down barriers.

Ice Princess

The ice-blonde, coolly elegant Hollywood star **Grace Kelly** (bi-wheel pictured on the next page) met Prince Rainier of Monaco on 6 May 1955. They married on **19 April 1956** when a series of apt (and almost-to-the-minute) Solar Arc Directions occurred. Here are a few, with quick one-line suggested interpretations.

1. Venus (ruler of the Descendant, natally in Libra conjunct a Scorpio Ascendant) conjuncts natal Mars in Scorpio – the powerful marriage union of Hollywood royalty to the Royal House of Grimaldi.

2. Uranus (natally in the 6th) conjuncts the natal Descendant in Taurus – Grace's relocation to Monaco and the abrupt end of her film career.

3. MC in Virgo quincunxes natal Uranus in the 6th in Aries – the sudden change in her daily life and routine; a new role in service to Monaco.

4. Neptune travelling through the 11th House and entering the sign of Libra (two months before the marriage) – the 'fairytale princess' and a marriage of social functions; the sacrifice of acting ambitions for the partnership.

It is said that Grace felt trapped in a marriage of convention and endless, boring social events, and that she *longed* to return to acting (Neptune).

Although I've yet to see much evidence that physical death can be predicted in one's own natal chart, the directions at the time of Princess Grace's death (in a car, apparently losing control while having a stroke) are very descriptive: Solar Arc Ascendant just past Saturn in Sagittarius in the 2nd, and directed Mars in the 3rd within orb to oppose Pluto (both rulers of her Ascendant). In the last year or so of her husband's life (2004–5), while his health was declining rapidly, Grace's chart was very active by Solar Arc: directed Descendant conjunct natal Pluto, Mars conjunct natal IC, and Neptune conjunct Sun.

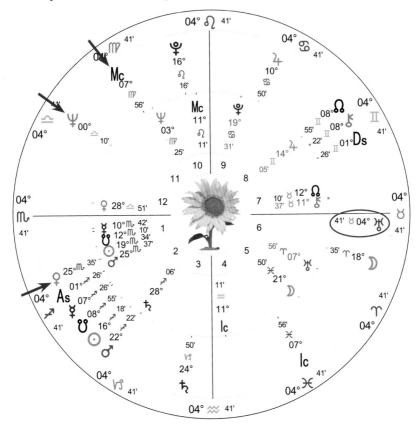

The Patsy's Decline

Chancellor **Gordon Brown**'s long wait to take over Blair's mantle as British PM came to an end on **27 June 2007** (the bi-wheel below is calculated for this date), after much speculation of a Blair–Brown 'inside deal' to pass over the reins of power. Whatever personal or professional enmity had been present between the pair, the timing was very apt for Brown astrologically: SA MC conjunct his natal Sun at the time he became leader. With the illegal war on Iraq and countless media spins, it seemed impossible that Blair would leave on a high note, but with the MC directing to Brown's Sun at the very first degree of Pisces, will this arrangement be recorded in the history books as a set-up for Brown to be the patsy (Pisces) for the Blair Years? A year later, in late July 2008, some MPs openly called on Brown to resign. This so-called 'Lancashire Plot' occurred when Solar Arc Pluto directed to his Descendant. At the time of his 2010 election defeat, MC ruler Saturn was at 29° Scorpio and the Sun was at 29° Aries – classic 'script changing' directions revealing the end of a major phase in his life.

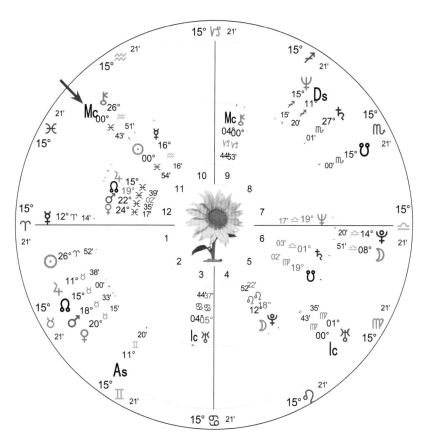

Part Three: Shadow Transits – A Hidden Forecasting Tool

In my client work, I accidentally stumbled across a tool that I later called a 'Shadow Transit' and now use frequently. We astrologers can, at times, be a little bit too generous with orbs, particularly in forecasting work, but I started to wonder why clients were coming (or returning) to see me at age 31-32 with the same issues they had at their Saturn Return (at 29). This often came with the cry, 'You told me it would all be over two years ago!' Inaccurate and a little unfair, but... This 'repetition' was happening long after the planet had moved beyond a reasonable orb of influence. I started to realize that the *Saturn Return ain't over till the Shadow Saturn Return*, which occurs two to three years later, has been completed. But more on that in a moment.

I always wondered what the difference would be between a transit to a natal position and a transit to a Solar Arc-directed position. Is one more important? Is it a case of either/or? When I asked around, the reply was, simply and unsatisfactorily, 'Ah yes, that's interesting.' And the matter was left dangling. Only my dear friend and colleague Melanie Reinhart had an opinion (on transits to natal and progressed planets) that answered some of my questions. Melanie saw the period between, for example, a transit over natal Uranus and progressed Uranus as an intensification and elongation of the transit process, where it stretches the trail and 'echoes' the theme through that period of time.

I didn't (and haven't yet) come across astrologers who had a theory on transits to Solar Arc positions or used this much in their work, so I began to research the idea. And, as is usually the case, clients brought the research to me – often in the form of an extended Saturn Return.

The Shadow Saturn Return

When transiting (TR) Saturn completes one lap of the zodiac and returns to its natal position, we experience a special Saturn transit: the landmark, coming-of-age Saturn Return. But in those 29 years, *Solar Arc* Saturn has directed forward roughly 29 degrees ahead of the natal Saturn (and usually into a new sign and a new house). It will then take the transiting Saturn in the sky a further 2.5 to 3 years to catch up with Solar Arc Saturn, which by then would have moved another 2.5 to 3 degrees (1 degree for each year). This is the Shadow Transit – a hidden event that links a planetary transit to the natal chart with a *later* planetary transit to the Solar Arc chart position.

I've discovered that these Shadow Transits repeat themes, events and feelings that transpired during the original transit to the natal horoscope. They give us another chance to tidy up unfinished business, another stab at an opportunity, or another possibility to recognize a pattern from the past – and to make different choices, if necessary.

If a client has not yet undergone the Shadow leg of the transit, we can use this tool to predict patterns that are likely to be repeated when it arrives. Knowing what happened during the transit-to-natal period enables us to understand the themes that might be revisited when that transiting planet finally catches up with the SA position. Of course, the length of time it will take to catch up depends on the transiting planet, so it may not happen in our lifetime. (We know, for example, that in an average life span, Pluto won't travel further than one-third around the horoscope.)

In her early 30s, 'Anna' arrived for an astrology-palmistry consultation in April 2005, during the transit of Saturn conjunct SA Saturn (her Shadow Saturn Return). Natally, Saturn was in Gemini in the 8th House (by Placidus and Equal Houses) and formed the handle of a bucket pattern. Saturnian issues of privacy and respect, emphasized by the planet's 8th House position, assumed even greater importance with her natal Moon in Capricorn and a Scorpio Ascendant. Treading carefully, and before discussing her current situation, I asked Anna what had happened during her original Saturn Return. She explained that her partner had had an affair and hurried back to confess all, leaving Anna to deal with the knowledge of a betrayal and the burden of a remorseful confession.

Arguably, given Saturn in Gemini in the 8th House, one message of the Saturn Return might have been to voice (Gemini) deep or volatile feelings such as betrayal (8th House) to process (mutable) this experience (Saturn) and communicate (Gemini) a range of Saturn/8th House issues. In *The Twelve Houses*, Howard Sasportas writes, 'The 8th House yields the opportunity to reexamine the connection between present relationship issues and those problems encountered with the mother and father early in life... The ruins and rubble from childhood are excavated in the 8th House... The gift of the 8th House is greater self-knowledge and self-mastery, freeing us to continue our journey renewed, less encumbered by unnecessary baggage.'[4] But my client had said nothing to her partner at the time and, in her words, 'just buried it'.

Now, in April 2005, she sat with me in my office undergoing the final leg of her Shadow Saturn Return, which occurred one sign and house on: in Cancer in the 9th House. I asked her if there were any links between the events of her first Saturn Return and her current situation, possibly with a 9th House (travel/education) or Cancerian (home/family/motherhood) theme. There were. She and her partner had been discussing whether to start a family, but my client had gone abroad (9th House) for a holiday on her own in August 2004 (the first hit) and had begun an affair with another man. When she returned, she kept silent about the holiday romance. When asked if anything occurred during the second hit (January 2005), Anna replied, 'I went back and spent another week with him.' I mentioned that the final hit would happen in mid-May 2005, just a few weeks away, and Anna smiled nervously. She had already booked another trip for a week during that period. The Shadow Saturn Return brought up the same issues but with a different emphasis (sign) and in another arena (house).

We spent much of the remaining time discussing the possibilities of exploring and articulating her natal Saturn in Gemini in the 8th. It is at this point that the astrologer feels privileged to be engaged in a process that is meaningful and empowering to both parties; it is not a matter of 'getting it right' and impressing clients with accurate past dates. When a dialogue is opened, it is more pertinent to ask, 'Where do we go with this information *now*?'

Publishing

I was able to look at my own Saturn Return (in Gemini in the 12th near the Ascendant) and make this connection, too. I had been publishing my own and others' astrology books from the age of 24, but at 27 I signed a contract with a major publisher to produce my first book on palmistry (not surprisingly, Gemini is highlighted frequently in the charts of hand-readers). The writing process had been a therapeutic joy, but the editing proved to be a struggle. I was greatly looking forward to the editing process (my work being shaped and moulded by the sort of editor a writer dreams of) but discovered that the book didn't really have an editor, just a proofreader, who managed to add a few hundred mistakes of her own to the manuscript! I rectified as many of these as I could see and hoped the publisher would incorporate them in time for the printing.

When the book was published during my once-only Saturn Return hit in May–June 2002, it contained even more errors. I was livid at the shoddiness of the work and how it would reflect on me. By speaking out and being unhappy with the mistakes I had encountered, I had become a 'difficult' author. The publisher corrected most of the errors in the second print run later that year, but I took the opportunity to sign with another publisher when the chance arose.

I wrote a second palmistry book, and the editing process was again stressful, as I seemed to be the only one who wanted the book to be as error-free as possible! It was published during my Shadow Saturn Return. I can't imagine the Saturn/12th House 'lesson' of letting go of the control-freak side of my character was fully learned during either transit because the experiences made me realize that I needed greater control over my work and reputation!

After seeing this in my own chart, I began to research the idea of connecting current Shadow Transits to events in the past. As an astrologer with a Gemini Ascendant, it's my experience that if you can help the client to link patterns that occur in different areas or times in their life, they're able to step away and look objectively at their situation and see those patterns at work clearly.

The Iron Lady

The chart for former UK Prime Minister **Margaret Thatcher** (bi-wheel opposite) makes captivating reading and is a master class in forecasting, perhaps because her natal Saturn in Scorpio on the Ascendant depicts a controlled, humourless Iron Lady who was famously 'not for turning'. As PM, she was an unyielding conservative with a strong work ethic, and her agenda was to restore her country to its glory days as a middle-class and prosperous Victorian nation (her Moon is conjunct Neptune on a Virgo Midheaven): 'Thatcher has taken her early life and used it as a touchstone to identify the old fashioned values that she holds, admires and would like to see restored.'[5] Her planets in Libra can be heard here: 'The codes of right and wrong lie at the bottom of every decision... They account for her inflexibility... and for the lack of imagination or real interest in debate.'[6]

Saturn transits or directions are often pivotal times in a politician's career. During Thatcher's second Saturn Return and the planet's passage over her Ascendant (January–April and September–October 1984), she faced two of her sternest tests while in office (famously dubbed her 'acid reign' by writer Quentin Crisp). First, there was the year-long (from March 1984) coal miners' strike (surely a fitting illustration of a Saturn Return over her Scorpio Ascendant). This was followed by a narrow escape from an assassination attempt[7] by the terrorist IRA – another apt example of the transit and its ties with her natal chart.[8]

In October and November 1990, while experiencing her *Shadow* Saturn Return, she was vulnerable again. Transiting Saturn had reached SA Saturn and

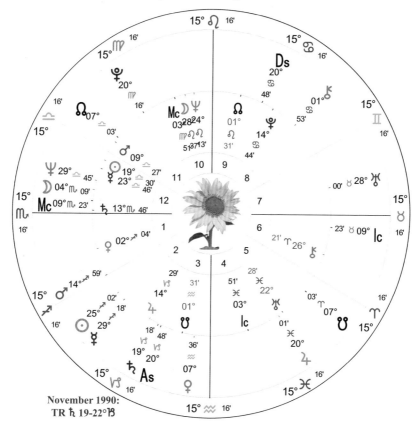

November 1990:
TR ♄ 19-22°♑

SA Ascendant, now both in Capricorn. (By then, SA Saturn–Ascendant had directed 65°, so the transit took more than six years to finally catch up.) The bi-wheel is calculated for **22 November 1990**, when Thatcher resigned over conflicts with key members of her Cabinet concerning European integration and a single currency, as well as the poll tax (a government house tax deemed unfair by much of the UK). A leadership challenge and lack of support from her Cabinet (Capricorn) had been the deciding factors in her resignation. (Note SA Saturn squares the Sun in Libra and SA Mars is quincunx Pluto at this time, too.)

Feed the World

Bob Geldof's natal chart (pictured opposite with his directions for **6 July 2005**) speaks volumes about his charitable work, as well as the lofty role to which he has been elevated: the front man for a rock band who suddenly became immersed in raising money for famine relief, and later became a media entrepreneur and political activist. The Sun in Libra is straddled by Mercury, Saturn and Neptune, opposed by Jupiter in Aries. This axis describes a musician who realized that he had a higher calling to make a difference to those who were starving to death in Ethiopia. Neptune relates to the human condition that recognizes charity, inspiration, compassion and suffering, and in Mercury–Saturn, we have an authoritative spokesman for justice and the restoration of equal rights (Libra). Jupiter in Aries opposing these planets suggests a zealous, idealistic and well-intentioned crusader. But wherever there's Jupiter, there's also the temptation to believe one's own publicity, to adopt the godlike status bestowed by others, and cut corners in an attempt to keep the gold plate from peeling off one's reputation. In short, Jupiter's challenge is to embrace and maintain *integrity*.

In late 1984, as TR Pluto hovered near his Midheaven (MC), Geldof saw TV reports of starvation in Ethiopia.[9] This awareness of famine (Pluto) profoundly changed his direction, reputation and world perspective (MC). Whether Geldof's MC is in late Libra or early Scorpio, either ruler (Venus or Mars) is in Virgo, a sign related to health, (mal)nutrition and victims (the small and overlooked). Geldof enlisted the help of celebrity friends (Jupiter) to form Band Aid, which raised money through the song 'Do They Know It's Christmas?', released in December 1984. Famously, Geldof said during the Live Aid TV transmission (13 July 1985), 'We need your f**king money! People are dying *now*.'

Twenty years later, Geldof planned Live 8 (2 July 2005), which was a concert to 'Make Poverty History', and The Long Walk to Justice (**6 July 2005**), in which Geldof called for leaders to cancel debt and to make aid/trade equal for all (the Mercury–Saturn conjunction in Libra). During both events, TR Pluto was at 22° Sagittarius, conjunct his SA MC (and natal Ascendant). The MC, once in Libra, was now in Sagittarius (the *long walk* to *justice*).

But on this occasion, the Long Walk idea was less practicable, as he urged one million people to descend on Edinburgh during the G8 political summit being held in Scotland. When asked where people would stay, he responded that

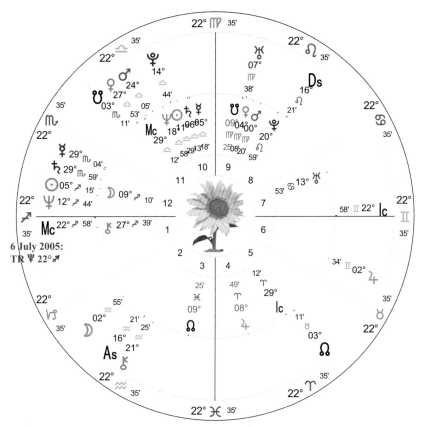

they should knock on the doors of strangers, who should accommodate them. At the time, he was accused of compromising the cause and supporting political agendas, and was criticized as an egotistical figure who set himself up as a messiah (Jupiter/Sagittarius).

Interestingly, at the same time, Geldof had another Shadow Transit: TR Neptune on his SA Ascendant. The original event (when transiting Neptune hit his natal Ascendant at 22° Sagittarius in late 1981) was when his band, The Boomtown Rats, hit an all-time low in popularity.

From Peter Pan to Pied Piper?

In May 1992, teenager **Jordan Chandler** (bi-wheel on the next page) met superstar recluse Michael Jackson. Within 18 months, news of his sleepovers and his accusations of molestation were to rock Jackson's life and tarnish, in many people's eyes, the singer's reputation as a fundraiser and supporter of underprivileged children. The world wanted to know if Peter Pan had turned into an abusive Pied Piper at his Neverland home.

I'm not convinced that the natal horoscope can show innocence or guilt, but it certainly describes the various scripts that we can act out, depending on numerous other factors (gender, society, privilege, race, generation, etc.). A more interesting question to pose, perhaps, is: can we see powerful, abusive or reclusive male figures 'written' in Jordy's script? And what of unusual friendships? Well, consider the Sun on the Ascendant in Capricorn closely square Pluto, Mars–Jupiter in the 8th, and Venus in Aquarius tightly square Uranus in Scorpio.

Chandler began his sleepovers at Neverland in March 1993. The scandal erupted between 20-22 August 1993, and an out-of-court settlement was reached between Jackson and the Chandler family on 25 January 1994. During this period, transiting Neptune and Uranus travelled over Jordy's natal Sun–Ascendant. The Neptune transit to Sun–Ascendant in Capricorn (which is squared natally by Pluto in Libra) depicted his contact and close relationship with a male superstar who introduced him to a seductive, glamorous lifestyle. It would suggest the alleged blurring and overstepping of friendship boundaries and the resulting tabloid sensationalism and media frenzy. The scandal brought accusations of

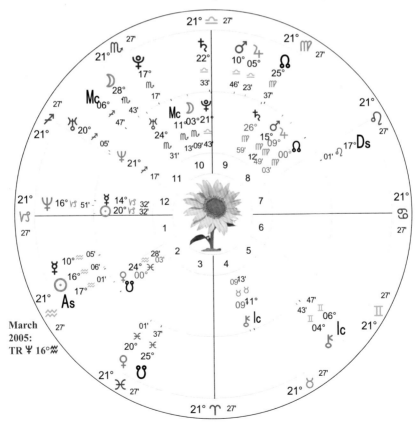

dishonesty and extortion against Jordy and his father (the Sun), and during this confusing, disorientating time, Jordy's contact with both his father and Jackson came to an abrupt end (TR Uranus – breaks – and Neptune – losses).

Ultimately, and regardless of the truth, Jordy's silence was bought and he went into hiding. His whereabouts were shrouded in mystery; he has never spoken out publicly and has only been photographed occasionally by paparazzi, usually in disguise or wearing dark sunglasses (note the Scorpio MC).

What of his chart during Jackson's second trial in early 2005? Surely there must be a Shadow Transit occurring. There was talk of forcing Jordy out of hiding to testify against his former friend. Would he or wouldn't he show? And if he did turn up, what on earth would he say under oath? The chart opposite is set for **1 March 2005**. Again, Neptune was conjunct his Sun and Ascendant, but this time it was their SA directed positions at 16-17° Aquarius. As it turned out, in Neptunian fashion, Jordy wasn't called, made no comment, and was alleged to have fled the country during the trial. (On 25 June 2009, Michael Jackson died suddenly. Jordy's SA Neptune was conjunct his natal Ascendant and was still in orb when his father Evan committed suicide on 5 November 2009.)

Some Clients' Stories

During my consultations, there's usually at least one occasion when Shadow Transit connections are made. One client, 'Larissa', had TR Uranus on her SA Mercury at 15° Pisces. I asked her what had happened the first time around (when TR Uranus conjoined natal Mercury at 10° Aquarius in the 2nd House). Back then, out of the blue (Uranus), an eccentric architect friend (Mercury in Aquarius) had offered her work space in his building for a minimal fee. At the start of her art career, this had helped Larissa's finances enormously. Now, during the Shadow Transit, the charitable friend had come back into the picture with another building space and another offer – this time free of charge (Pisces).

Another client had TR Pluto conjunct her Moon–Neptune–IC in Scorpio when her father was dying of cancer. Part of the stress during this time was keeping his illness secret from her mother, who was herself incapacitated. When TR Pluto moved to 0° Capricorn in early 2008, it was now sitting on my client's SA Moon in the 5th House. Under this transit, she began a difficult separation from her long-term partner. During the consultation, she said, 'This situation has been even more painful than losing my father to cancer.'

During a consultation, a client and I discussed her TR Neptune conjunct SA Jupiter in Aquarius. The original Neptune transit to her natal Jupiter occurred in Capricorn when, under the heavy weight of expectation, she had given up (Neptune is linked to resignation) just before her finals at university (Jupiter in Capricorn). At the time of our meeting, she was training to be a professional astrologer but had decided not to take the final qualifying examinations (SA Jupiter was now in Aquarius). The outcome of the consultation was that she chose to stick with her training, and I'm delighted to say she passed her exams.

Disgraced Champion

With Saturn on the MC in Leo, athlete and Olympic champion **Marion Jones** (bi-wheel opposite) was held up as a shining example of blue ribbon (and gold medal) achievement. But Saturn holds us accountable, and a tight natal square from Uranus suggests a reversal of her Saturn–MC standing. Here's a chronology of events during her Saturn Return (at the MC) and the resultant Shadow Transits:

1. February 2006: After being accused of taking steroids, Jones wins/settles a defamation lawsuit, but the International Olympic Committee says it will investigate further – TR Saturn Return and TR Saturn conjunct MC.

2. 5 October 2007: Jones retires, admitting steroid use and lying in a federal investigation – TR Saturn conjunct SA Saturn (Shadow Saturn Return).

3. December 2007 to January 2008: Jones is formally stripped of her Olympic medals in December and banned from competing; in January, she is sentenced to six months in prison – TR Saturn conjunct SA MC.

4. 7 March 2008: She reports to the prison – Shadow Saturn Return again.

Saturn–MC conjunctions (natally or by transit) are occasionally 'fall from grace' aspects. And with a Leo MC, the impact of a male Svengali on Jones' life is likely. (There are a number of other signs in the horoscope that act as significators for her life events, and remarkably, two of her partners have been involved in drug scandals – note the Descendant ruler Venus is square to Neptune.)

I find it interesting that, at the time of her ban and public condemnation (the chart opposite is set for **5 October 2007**), Marion's Solar Arc MC was closely conjunct Florence Griffith-Joyner's natal 12th House Moon–Pluto conjunction at 6° and 7° Virgo. Flo Jo's extraordinary (and much debated) 1988 Olympic gold medals and world records had been the inspiration for a teenage Marion Jones.

Final Words

When trying to anticipate how a transit to a Solar Arc Directed planet is working in a client's life (possible themes, experiences, areas of life and events), I now track the date of the original transit to the natal chart and ask, 'What happened back then?' More often than not, the client recalls an event that has a direct link to current circumstances. But the new aspect will usually be in a different sign or house, so there's a twist in the interpretation. It's the same visitor at the door, but in a different costume.

Try it out yourself. Play detective and look at your Shadow Saturn Return or other transits (not just conjunctions) to Solar Arc positions, and make the links to past transits/events. It may be a repeat, 'here we go again' experience but in a different setting and with different players. With the benefit of hindsight, we can make useful, meaningful links between past and present conditions that can empower our clients, and ourselves, to make informed choices about our lives.

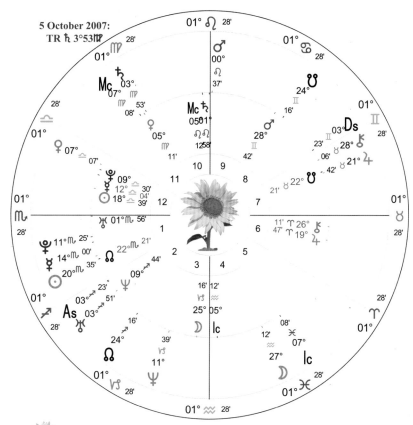

Part Four: A Note on Forecasting

Forecasting is about helping the client become attuned to the planetary cycles and rhythms of their lives. Rather than trying to predict what will happen, most astrologers work to help clients become aware of these cycles/celestial rhythms. By recognizing the season they're in, clients can embrace the current climate. Astrologers articulate the processes taking place and the types of feelings the client is likely to have, and the associations they'll make because of their natal chart. The natal chart's major configurations and hard aspects reveal the life stories we're born to encounter (these can manifest as developmental processes, actual events or even non-personal situations we encounter in the world around us), but we benefit by engaging in a dialogue with clients and asking for *context* to understand the stage they are at in life, their perception and involvement. We also need to play detective: to find out what happened last time during the same or similar transit/direction, to understand who or what could be represented by the planet in forecasting. Forecasting best describes the processes/feelings/reactions rather than actual events (with hindsight, events can be 'seen' in meaningful ways). Arguably, the only 'fated' (determined) part is the horoscope construct itself, as it is based upon a moment in time which we cannot change (from which a set of predictable and unchangeable transits/progressions/directions follow).

I use a simple method to forecast I call 'Define & Connect'. In order to get to the heart of a transit/direction, it is essential to break down the parts involved, understand the natal chart and the energy of the particular transit/direction.

1. *Define* the activator (the transiting/directing planet). This is the energy in the forecast. What is its astrological meaning? In general, what does it *do* and what does it represent in us and in the world around us?

2. *Connect* this planet to the natal chart. Identify its natal sign and house placement (plus key aspects and house rulerships) to get a picture of how it behaves, responds and functions in this particular chart. This is the 'memory' – a storehouse of lifelong associations – triggered every time this planet transits/directs.

3. *Define* the planet being activated (aspected). In general, what does this planet represent in us and in the world? What are its principal meanings/ associations in astrology?

4. *Connect* this planet to the natal chart. Look at its sign and house position (plus key aspects and house rulerships). This is the area of the person and their life that is being opened up for some change and transformation.

Notes

1. Solar Arc Directions can also be moved backwards, and are known as Converse Directions. These are essentially the same as regular, forward-moving directions except the planet/point doing the directing is swapped (instead of point A reaching point B, point B goes back to point A – the Ascendant can be directed forwards to Mercury in the 1st House at age 17, or Mercury can move back to the Ascendant by Converse Direction at age 17).

2. This is where directions differ greatly from progressions. The progressed Moon moves very fast (between 12–15° per progressed year – covering much more ground than the directed Moon), while progressed Neptune and Pluto barely move more than a few degrees during an average lifetime. With directions, there is much greater outer planetary movement and during an average lifetime the outer planets (along with every other planet/angle) can direct through up to 3–4 signs and 3–4 houses. There is also no likelihood of a planet slowing down and moving retrograde as it can do in the progressed chart. With progressions, the inner planets are given more importance (the progressed Moon is a particularly important timer/trigger), but with directions, *every* planet/angle has (potentially) the same importance/weighting. Note, however, that the Sun and the MC move at the same rate in both the Solar Arc method and the progressed chart, and thus will each be the same degree in both systems.

3. The same can be applied to a planet moving into a new house. Try this out with your preferred house system. I've been using Equal Houses for about fifteen years, and every planet moving house also aspects the Ascendant/Descendant axis degree.

4. Howard Sasportas, *The Twelve Houses*, Flare Publications, 2007, p.61.

5. N. Wapshott and G. Brock, *Thatcher*, Futura, 1983.

6. Penny Junor, *Margaret Thatcher: Wife, Mother, Politician*, Sidgwick & Jackson, 1983.